DISCARD

# Gaining Support
# for Your School

The Practicing Administrator's Leadership Series
Jerry J. Herman and Janice L. Herman, Editors

ROADMAPS
TO SUCCESS

# Other Titles in This Series Include:

(see back cover for additional titles)

# Gaining Support for Your School

## Strategies for Community Involvement

Donna M. Schmitt
Jaclynn C. Tracy

CORWIN PRESS, INC.
A Sage Publications Company
Thousand Oaks, California

*For information address:*

Corwin Press, Inc.
A Sage Publications Company
2455 Teller Road
Thousand Oaks, California 91320
email: order@corwin.sagepub.com

SAGE Publications Ltd.
6 Bonhill Street
London EC2A 4PU
United Kingdom

SAGE Publications India Pvt. Ltd.
M-32 Market
Greater Kailash I
New Delhi 110 048 India

Printed in the United States of America

**Library of Congress Cataloging-in-Publication Data**

Schmitt, Donna M.
    Gaining support for your school : strategies for community
involvement / Donna M. Schmitt, Jaclynn C. Tracy.
        p.   cm. — (Roadmaps to success)
    Includes bibliographical references (pp. 52-56).
    ISBN 0-8039-6410-2 (alk. paper)
        1. Community and school—United States—Handbooks, manuals, etc.
I. Tracy, Jaclynn C.   II. Title.   III. Series.
LC215.S35   1996
370.19'31—dc20                                                    95-43338

This book is printed on acid-free paper.

# Contents

# Foreword

Donna Schmitt and Jaclynn Tracy have produced a brief book that places great emphasis on getting broader community involvement with schools in order to improve the environment for students. They hold that school-community collaboration is more important than ever because of the reluctance of citizens to vote for higher taxes for school operations and because of the multitude of criticisms about the level of student achievement.

The book deals with the requirement for schools to change and the need to rebuild confidence in the schools. The authors stress how important it is that school leaders commit themselves to involving their schools with the broader community in the future and offer, through a six-step process, strategies and tactics to accomplish this goal.

*Gaining Support for Your School* is clearly designed as a handbook for practitioners. In addition to the wealth of information provided in the book's chapters, an annotated bibliography of primary sources is included to assist the reader in locating additional helpful information regarding school-community involvement.

JERRY J. HERMAN
JANICE L. HERMAN
*Series Co-Editors*

# About the Authors

**Donna M. Schmitt** has been an administrator for 14 years at Eastern Michigan University, serving as the Associate Dean of the College of Education, Department Head of Leadership & Counseling, and Director of the Center for Community Education. She is a Professor of Educational Leadership in the Department of Leadership and Counseling, where she teaches courses in leadership theory, community education, supervision of instruction, evaluation of educational services, administration of higher education, and women in leadership.

Schmitt earned a bachelor of arts degree from The College of Racine (Wisconsin), and master of arts and doctor of education degrees from Western Michigan University in Community Education and Instructional Leadership. Areas of Schmitt's research include leadership styles, women in leadership, and integration of community education into the K-12 curriculum.

**Jaclynn C. Tracy** is Assistant Professor of Educational Leadership in the Department of Leadership and Counseling at Eastern Michigan University. Prior to coming to the university, she was an administrator in the public schools of Michigan for 18 years, serving as the Director of Community Education in Chelsea School District and Coordinator of Community Education for Bedford Public Schools. She earned her bachelor's, master's, and specialist degrees at Eastern Michigan University. Her doctor of philosophy degree is in Adult and Continuing Education from Michigan State University.

Tracy's areas of instruction include school-community relations, community education, and adult education, and she is currently the Director of the Internship Program for Educational Leadership. Her research has investigated alternative delivery systems for educational programming especially as related to adult instruction.

# Introduction

In an era of declining resources and rising expectations, public schools today find themselves competing for allocations from a shrinking pool of resources. Constituencies have become more and more reluctant to tax themselves for schools that the public finds, based on individual perceptions, to be remote and removed from day-to-day living. When only 30% of the adult population in a typical community have school-age children, 70% of potential voters question cost-benefit ratios when school-tax time arrives and frequently decide that it is not to their benefit to bear additional costs for schools.

We frequently hear critics of schools citing the need to improve student achievement levels, provide more relevant learning experiences, and have a curriculum that addresses current societal needs. When high school graduates cannot read the manual in the shop, when teen clerks at the fast-food place have difficulty making change, or when results of state and national achievement tests do not meet expectations, the public responds with demands for change and accountability. These demands have been in the form of calls for schools of choice, charter schools, home schooling, and the privatization of education (Bracey, 1994).

More and more we note that the community views itself as the consumer of education; that is, the community believes that it ought to receive some "goods" in exchange for the money it provides to the schools. As noted, when individuals feel that they are not getting anything worthwhile for their school money, negativism and lack of support result. Only through the development of mutual ownership of schools by professionals and the community can we reverse this type of thinking. Recent studies of collaborative efforts (Fullan, 1993; Padak, Peek, Borthwick, & Shaklee, 1993; Sarason, 1990) have demonstrated that increasing the involvement of the community in the schools has resulted in increasing the support for schools, support by way of dollars and support by way of commitment. This involvement begins with the development of a two-way communication process that assesses needs and coordinates resources. We must get our community *in* schools, *involved* in schools, and *invested* in schools.

The need for change in the way we have been "doing business" in public schools is explored in chapter 1. The chapter describes various ways to ensure the equity and access that are the hallmark of public schools while also rebuilding public confidence and support for these schools. Proven successes based on the experiences of school districts that have implemented programs to foster community involvement are discussed.

Chapter 2 looks at a structure for community involvement that begins with new understandings and commitments on the part of governing boards. Six components are identified that can serve as a guide for action plans to move from confrontation to collaboration.

Chapter 3 reviews specific programs that describe the community's new role and involvement in schools, including volunteer programs, school-community partnerships, community service learning, school-to-work programs, and full-service schools. Strategies for implementation and curricular implications of these programs are also discussed.

Chapter 4 evaluates specific programs that describe the school's new role and involvement in the community, including supplemental academic, enrichment, and recreation programs for children and similar academic, enrichment, and recreation programs for the adult members of the community. Examples of both programs and services are cited.

Chapter 5 presents school leaders with the call to action necessary for successful school-community involvement in the future. Guidelines for action and strategies for implementation of enhanced school-community relations are noted, including specific applications.

This handbook is intended to provide the school leader with both a rationale and a roadmap for developing realistic community involvement in schools. The annotated bibliography provides additional practical resources for assisting in this crucial process of rebuilding support for public schools.

# The Need
# for Change: Involving
# Community and Schools

**W**riting a decade ago, Marvin Cetron (1985), the forecaster, stated: "No issue confronting schools today will have as great an impact on the future of education as the question of funding" (p. 78). With the 20/20 vision of hindsight, we can say that Cetron's conclusion and the focus on finances were exactly on target but were more symptomatic than causal. For, although the funding of schools is indeed the rallying cry of much of what has happened in public education in the last 10 years, it is but one aspect of the turbulent state of the profession in the 1990s. Funding for schools has been the weapon that communities have used to call attention to more fundamental concerns. Underneath the money issues lie questions regarding the very purpose of public education and its obligation to serve local communities. At the same time, as Sergiovanni (1994) states, "The need for community is universal. A sense of belonging, of continuity, of being connected to others and to ideas and values that make our lives meaningful and significant—these needs are shared by all of us" (p. xiii).

## Changing Demographics

In the recent past, it was not difficult to see that the major social institutions in our communities were clearly identified with particular, and interrelated, functions. Families, large and extended, passed down traditions and the values embedded in them. The churches expanded upon these traditions and grounded them in a belief system. Commercial enterprise provided for the transaction of business based on these values, while government developed the legal framework for them. And the schools were expected to induct students into educational realms replete with the "wisdom of the ages" that spawned the values. Because the majority of the households in the community had school-age children, it was not hard to see the centrality of the role of the schools in this social structure, nor the obvious sense of need and support such a position would engender from the community for these schools. Schools were personally very meaningful for most adults living in such a community and time.

The community of the 1990s, however, is quite different from its predecessor. The majority of households in the typical community today do not have children in school. In fact, only slightly more than 35% of American adults are categorized as parents of school-age children (National Opinion Research Corporation, 1993), and only 32% are parents of children who attend public schools (Elam & Rose, 1995, p. 56). Smaller families, more singles, geographic mobility, and an aging population have dramatically changed the demographics of our communities (Hodgkinson, 1992). Without any primary focus for much of the adult population in the community, the schools have lost their centrality and essential connectedness for many of these adults. The personalized meaning that once characterized schools and their functions is missing for the majority of those whose financial support is necessary for these schools.

## Institutions and Change

Communities today are perfecting the fine art of being customers. Ours is a service-driven economy with a new culture for "doing business." Institutions and organizations, manufacturers and service agencies of every sort, from automobile makers to hospitals, are acutely aware of the need to address the consumer as customer. Customers are people who can (and will) take their business elsewhere if they feel their needs are not being met. These needs include the obvious need for quality goods or services, as well as the accompanying needs for respect and concern for the customer's well-being in the process. It is this latter set of needs—the personalizing of the process—that makes the consumer a customer.

So it is with public education and communities. Today's schools must focus on an approach to doing business that views community members—all community members—not just as consumers of schooling, but as customers of education.

> The real challenge for school administrators in the 1990s and the twenty-first century will not be keeping the building clean, completing the paperwork, and making sure the busses are running on time, but rather the challenge will be to rethink and re-create the school as an institution that is responsive to life in the twenty-first century. (Kowalski & Reitzug, 1993, p. 274)

As a result of this need for reestablishing personalized meaning with the schools, we have seen the rise of two phenomena in educational arenas—responsiveness and competition. Some public schools have been quite astute in identifying the real disconnectedness fueling the school-funding revolts and have seen the need to be responsive. They have reached out, identified needs, and used resources to address these needs in a way that provides personal meaning for community members. In other communities, where this has not been done, other organizations have developed in competition with the schools, organizations that do address educational needs in customer-focused, personally meaningful, ways.

Another hallmark of contemporary communities is the desire for convenience and "user-friendliness" in the consumption of goods and services. Responsive schools, like other service providers, address the schedules of households with full-time wage earners, schedules with multiple demands on personal time and attention. Community members seek those contacts and opportunities that are short, concise, and personalized experiences at convenient times and in easily reached locations, rather than extended commitments during traditional working hours in distant settings.

To be truly relevant to the needs of today's communities, schools must make a conscious decision to find out the new expectations of these communities and devise new delivery systems to meet these expectations. In this way, the educational institution will reestablish its centrality in the hearts and minds of the educational customer of the future.

## The Public School

As we seek the best avenues to serve our communities in the public schools, there are a number of elements embedded in our heritage that can and must be used for the foundation of our new approach. The education of children is, of course, a primary purpose, and foremost among the principles guiding us are equity and access. Public schools, by definition, must be build upon the premise that education is available to all and delivered to all. As Goals 2000 restates, the unique American belief in universal education is one of the strongest elements of what communities today are seeking from their public schools (U.S. Department of Education, 1994).

The scenario that schools have been less and less able, for various reasons, to deliver on this promise of equity and access has triggered the erosion of public confidence in these schools. Communities want their schools to meet expectations (customer needs), and as the demographic makeup of the community and its needs change, so must the schools.

Directly related to the confidence issue is the support issue. When people experience direct and personal benefits from an agency, they are more likely to provide the funding necessary to ensure the continuation of the service.

In developing new configurations to meet new community needs, public schools can provide a variety of alternatives, as the needs of the community warrant. Such alternatives take a long and realistic look at the barriers to change that are involved in current practices and programs, and foster "thinking outside the box" of traditional schooling and education. "To change, we have to challenge practices that have always appeared sensible" (Sergiovanni, 1994, p. 1). Opportunities for alternative programs and settings, for more "choices" in delivery and content, must be viewed in light of the new community and its expectations.

## Community Schools: A Proven Response

One educational delivery model that has been quite successful in identifying community expectations and building a responsive program based on customer involvement is the community schools movement. In those communities where the model has been fully implemented, schools have flourished through strong community support, both in terms of commitment and in terms of finances. These schools have developed programs and practices based on the premise that the schools are catalysts for addressing the broad educational needs of the community.

Examples of schools and communities that have embraced the community schools model in recent times include both urban and rural areas, such as Flint, Michigan; St. Louis Park, Minnesota; Brockton, Massachusetts; San Diego, California; Eureka, Montana; and Yelm, Washington. Information about, training in, and technical assistance regarding the community schools concept are available from the National Center for Community Education in Flint, Michigan: (810) 238-0463. These schools have demonstrated increased learning opportunities for both children and adults, have enhanced K-12 curriculum through school-community partnerships, and have expanded the roles for citizen involvement in decision making.

Many of the school districts that identify themselves as having "community schools" further identify the philosophy of community education as the base for the program. A commonly accepted definition of community education is that of Minzey and LeTarte (1994):

Community Education is a philosophical concept which serves the entire community by providing for all of the educational needs of all of the community members. It uses the local school to serve as a catalyst for bringing community resources to bear on community problems in an effort to develop a positive sense of community, improve community living, and develop the community process toward the end of self-actualization. (p. 58)

As public schools approach the 21st century, new expectations on the part of changing communities require innovative responses. Building on the successes of the past, ensuring equity and access, and striving to meet emerging needs, schools will enjoy the support that comes from a satisfied "education customer." A description of the structure of this new approach to education and the specific elements guiding schools to effective action are discussed in chapter 2.

# A Structure
# for Community
# Involvement

**B**eing responsive to the emerging needs of the community requires the development of a new structure for community involvement. This responsiveness originates with a commitment at the policy level on the part of the schools and results in programs and processes that build a commitment at the support level on the part of the community.

> Strong community involvement in schools brings important benefits: additional resources, political support, opportunities for innovation and professional development, and increased student achievement. The degree of involvement will depend, however, on the model a school chooses. Consistent, high-level participation of parents and other community members is not likely to be achieved without planning. The principal, together with the management team, must provide leadership and delegate explicit responsibilities for managing participation. (Keith & Girling, 1991, pp. 275-276)

## Starting With New Commitments

Education policymakers must provide the impetus for community support through involvement in the schools. This is best done by working with the school staff members and community members to develop a vision for community involvement. In this vision, the rules, roles, and relationships of various constituent groups are defined; a plan to engage the community in ongoing dialogue relative to the expanded vision is developed; and, at the operational level, boards empower school leaders to pursue the vision. Policies and procedures ensure community involvement; programs make it a reality.

School governing boards committed to a vision of greater community involvement in the schools develop a service orientation as it relates to the schools' role and mission, show a commitment of support for lifelong learning, and provide leadership for collaboration. In addition, the following districtwide policies are either drafted or revised to reflect this new commitment to community involvement:

- Expanded community use of facilities
- Mandated community involvement in decision making, for example, school improvement teams, advisory councils, site-based management teams, and curriculum councils
- Enhanced communication systems with community
- Structured partnerships and interagency collaboration
- Organizational commitment to lifelong learning

Earlier we described a society that looks to the schools for support in meeting new challenges that face the child, the family, and the community. The schools address these challenges when they expand their view of service to include not only the K-12 child but also the family and the larger community. This expanded role and mission for service is inherent in the evolution of the public schools in a democratic society.

- Schools are publicly supported and have the potential for generating additional resources to meet expanded expectations.
- School district facilities represent a large financial investment in the community but are used only a fraction of the day and year for traditional school programming.
- Schools are adaptable for a wide variety of community uses and programs.
- Public schools are located in neighborhoods easily accessible to community members.
- Schools have strong community identities, with homes often selected on the basis of the location and quality of a school.
- Schools have an entrée into families and extended communities through children.
- School boundaries cut across political lines.
- Schools are often less affected by the abuses of politics. (Minzey & LeTarte, 1994)

One way to provide expanded service to the community is through support for lifelong learning. It is commonly accepted that education and training are lifelong processes. Schools support this concept via an expanded belief system that encourages and nurtures the learning process, whether it is through a schools-only program for adult students or through a collaborative venture joining the resources of schools and other organizations.

As the vision of schools expands to support an environment rich in community involvement, the roles and responsibilities of school personnel likewise expand.

- Teachers view parents and family as partners in the education process, extend their classrooms into the community, bring the community into the classroom, participate in shared decision making, and facilitate the learning process with a variety of community resources.
- Building principals provide leadership for shared decision making, support the expanded use of school and community facilities, join forces with other agencies sharing common goals, and use community resources to enhance student success at the classroom and building level.

- Central office administrators provide leadership for collaboration, generate and maintain support for lifelong learning programs and services, create opportunities for community involvement, and systematically communicate with the internal and external publics relative to the district's expanded mission.

Similarly, district budgets are also affected as a result of the expanded commitment to community involvement. Initial investments in personnel, program, and service costs are absorbed by the district. Often, the burden of excess expenditures is minimized in time by the fees generated through services and collaborative initiatives associated with greater community involvement in schools.

Decision making throughout the organization is enhanced by the involvement of the community. "Consultation, involvement, and group decision making are generally superior to individual decision making" (Keith & Girling, 1991, p. 135). Curriculum committees, site-based management and school improvement teams, local advisory councils, and interagency collaboratives are all examples of vehicles that provide community access to the schools and school access to the community.

## Components of the New Structure

Six major components constitute a guide for action to achieve increased community involvement and ownership in the schools. These six components are

- Enhancement of the K-12 curriculum
- Expanded use of community facilities
- Additional learning opportunities for youth
- Lifelong learning programs for adults
- Delivery and coordination of community services
- Community involvement in decision making. (Minzey & LeTarte, 1994)

## Enhancement of the K-12 Curriculum

The K-12 curriculum is central to the public school structure and to the mission of the schools. Community involvement in K-12 programming is achieved by using available resources to supplement the curriculum, making it richer and more relevant. This is accomplished through strong volunteer programs, school-community partnerships, the use of the community as the classroom, and other programs that, in effect, dissolve the walls between classroom and community. Examples of these programs may include community service learning opportunities, school-to-work initiatives, and full-service schools.

The scope of a program that supports community involvement in the schools is based on the needs of the school, its students and its curriculum, and the resources available within the community. Formal and informal relationships are established with area businesses and corporations, government and community agencies, civic organizations, institutions of higher education, and other community members. The key to successful programs is agreement upon mutual goals and objectives for a particular program or project.

Examples of this type of community involvement that enriches the K-12 curriculum include internship experiences and work-study opportunities, field trips, bringing "services" into schools, adopt-a-school programs, sponsorship of special events, articulation agreements, action research projects with higher education, and financial and human contributions in support of specific activities.

Implementation strategies and the curricular implications of such programs will be discussed in chapter 3. In addition, we will identify exemplary school sites.

## Expanded Use of Community Facilities

As the schools make the commitment to provide increased opportunities for lifelong learning programs and services, sites for program delivery become necessary. Schools, being readily available and accessible, are the logical choice for many of these programs. Most school facilities are used only a fraction of the available time. Board policies and internal staff support for community activities in the schools ensure the development of successful relationships, where an "open door" policy is sincerely and consistently practiced.

Besides public school facilities, most communities have other buildings and sites that can be used for the delivery of lifelong learning programs and services. A community facilities inventory can identify the availability of possible program sites, as well as the parameters for their use. Community facilities to be identified include

- Local, state, and federal government buildings
- Museums
- Libraries
- Business and industrial group sites
- Parks and recreation centers
- Institutions of higher education
- Hospitals
- Fire halls
- Union halls
- Churches
- Private schools

An example of extensive use of school facilities for community programs is found in Anchorage, Alaska. For more than 20 years, the Anchorage community has benefited from programs provided in the neighborhoods for people of all ages. Eighteen community schools facilitate outreach to the residents through year-round daytime and evening programs for both adults and youth.

Community facilities, including school buildings, are valued resources. Maximizing the use of such facilities for lifelong learning programs and services adds to the value of these resources and leads to increased commitment on the part of both school and community to the success of such programs.

### Additional Learning Opportunities for Youth

The goal of a learning society focuses on lifelong learning using resources of the school, family, and community "to educate people of all ages at all stages of their lives" (Decker & Decker, 1988, p. vi). With the explosion of knowledge and information that has occurred in recent times likely to continue and, indeed, grow every day, it is impossible to provide K-12 students with optimal learning opportunities in the traditional school-day format alone. Also, research has revealed that early intervention in the intellectual, physical, and social development of children greatly increases their potential for success (Ramey & Ramey, 1994). Schools extend and supplement the "school-day curriculum" by offering lifelong learning programs—academic, enrichment, and recreational—to all children in the community, including those of preschool age.

Early childhood education programs provide the stimulation necessary to sustain the natural desire to learn. In some communities, early childhood education opportunities through nonschool agencies are abundant; in others, this is not the case. Regardless of the situation in any particular community, school districts committed to the goal of lifelong learning must be involved in community-wide programming at some level for this age group. This involvement not only lays a solid foundation for future student achievement; it also restores the schools to the center of the learning cycle in the community. The school's role in the holistic development of the community's youth is established early in a child's life.

Educational programming for youth that is administered and/ or supported by schools is a necessity in the promotion of lifelong learning. Examples of programs that expand the school day, the school week, and the school year are "Super Saturday" enrichment programs, summer athletic and enrichment camps, before- and after-school child care programs, tutoring services, after-school enrichment and recreation activities, early childhood education programs, and alternative education opportunities. These types of programs are further defined and described in chapter 4.

### Lifelong Learning Programs for Adults

This component of the goals pursued by school districts that are committed to community involvement provides for services to the adults in the community similar to those offered for youth. A key factor here is that the learning needs of adults are recognized as being as important to the school and the community as are the learning needs of youngsters.

Focusing on the learning needs of parents in the community provides great support to the learning needs of their children, thus enhancing the K-12 program. However, "because a declining proportion of the electorate will have children in school, it will continue to be difficult to convince voters to spend more money on educational services that they perceive to have no direct benefit to them" (Keith & Girling, 1991, p. 12). Providing lifelong learning opportunities for both parents and adults who do not have children creates an additional basis for support for the schools.

Central to adult programming is the assessment of adult needs and the utilization of available resources to address these needs. Academic, enrichment, vocational, and recreational programming is the result. Such programs include high school completion, adult basic skill education, English as a Second Language for the foreign born, higher education courses, alternative education programs, avocational classes and activities, vocational-technical training opportunities, and community sports leagues and recreational programs.

As our population ages, the need for programming for senior citizens becomes more and more apparent. Intergenerational programs and other academic, enrichment, and recreational programs for this age group, as well as for younger adults, are described in chapter 4.

### Delivery and Coordination of Community Services

Critics of the expanded role for schools that is inherent in the commitment to lifelong learning and community involvement note that "schools can't do it all." The response to that argument is that support can and does come from agencies other than public schools. Comprehensive programs and services to meet community learning needs require a coordinated commitment from all organizations and agencies with a common interest—improvement of the community through education.

Most communities do not lack the services and resources required to meet their needs. What is lacking is an appropriate needs assessment, as well as the coordination of programs and services necessary to meet those needs (Minzey & LeTarte, 1994). Schools play an important leadership role in initiating both of these functions.

When maximizing existing community resources, the "c" words—cooperation, coalition building, coordination, collaboration, and communication—come into play. In providing leadership to this coordination function, school administrators ask the question, "Which agency in the community possesses the greatest expertise (for meeting the community need identified), and how will others support them in extending this program or service?" Most often it is a nonschool agency that is identified. The only time the school becomes the program agent is when a program or service to meet identified needs does not exist and the school is the most appropriate agency for providing the service.

A prime example of interagency collaboration is the "pro-family" initiative that is currently gaining momentum. The goal of this initiative is to expand the capacity of helping institutions, crisis intervention, and treatment services to meet the needs of families. Melaville, Blank, and Asayesh (1993) suggest a five-stage process for addressing these needs, and report the following characteristics of effective initiatives to change service delivery systems. Effective initiatives

- Are school-linked
- Are rooted in the community and closely connected to state government
- Use place-specific service delivery prototypes to create systems change
- Are data driven
- Are financially pragmatic
- Use new forms of interprofessional preservice and inservice education, training, and leadership development
- Use the collaborative's influence to engage all citizens in decisions about the social and economic well-being of children and families
- Balance the political and technical dimensions of systems change (p. 16)

The authors further state:

> Instead of following a cookbook, step-by-step approach, partners must find the most effective way to knit their local needs, resources and preferences into a purposeful plan. The challenge is to develop a process of working together that is flexible enough to allow adjustments to new circumstances, while staying focused on long-term goals. (p. 19)

The Madison Heights (Michigan) Community Roundtable is an excellent example of the synergy that develops when schools take the leadership to bring community resources together. The Roundtable is an ongoing structure for matching community resources with community needs; it has been serving the community for more than a decade. Membership includes two school districts, the chamber of commerce, business and industry, the municipal government, churches, parochial schools, service groups, and community agencies, who meet monthly to share information, identify needs, and develop leadership for collaborative action.

The actual location of the delivery of the services becomes the final challenge. The accessibility of neighborhood schools and local ownership of these facilities make the school buildings a logical choice. The goal is to meet the needs of the community in the "friendliest," most efficient manner possible.

### Community Involvement in Decision Making

Community support for schools is further developed by actively seeking community participation in decision-making processes, governance, and advocacy. People will support that which they have built. Schools have traditionally encouraged parent and community groups such as the PTA, booster clubs, and parent resource councils. With the new commitment to community involvement, schools add new avenues for input and sharing in decisions by including community representation on school improvement teams, site-based management committees, and task forces of all types. The school also establishes advisory committees to provide community input on programs and needs, and facilitates (or joins) interagency collaboratives focused on ensuring the shared decision making and resource allocation necessary for maximum community service and ownership.

Extensive use of the community advisory council for community involvement in decision making is evident in the Ankeny, Iowa School District. Beginning with a planning process that involved extensive surveying of community needs, community residents used the schools as the base for developing the advisory council, the vehicle then used to identify resources and needed programming. The success of this process resulted in a desire for trained leadership. As now employed, this leadership provides the day-to-day management for the delivery of programs and services under the direction of the council. The planning cycle continues through the use of the Ankeny Community Betterment Survey, which is conducted every 5 years, using volunteers to collect and tabulate information.

A note of caution about creating and using advisory committees or groups relates to the training for group work that members are given. It is counterproductive to organize such groups and simply give them tasks to accomplish without providing them with the necessary tools. The most important of these tools is the skill to function as a group, rather than as a collection of individuals. Johnson and Johnson (1994) note that "You are not born with group skills, nor do they magically appear when you need them. You have to learn them" (p. 48). Understanding group processes, knowing what are appropriate group member and group leadership functions, being able to demonstrate these functions, and committing to shared responsibility for the group are all vital to the group's success. It is imperative that time and training be dedicated to these topics at the very beginning of the group's work.

## Conclusion

As the world becomes a more demanding, frantic place to live, the needs of its inhabitants multiply. The old rules no longer apply; new rules must be written, learned, and applied. One possible reason that change is so threatening to most people is that change is a lonely process that almost invariably involves a sense of loss.

Although the community has always stood as the cornerstone of Americans' ability to deal with change, insulating us from loneliness and loss, these times call for a reexamination of exactly what that community should be. It is indeed a time of different faces and different needs. Schools have always played an important role in every community, and if the community is to remain the foundation of our ability to adapt, schools must rise to the challenge of change. For schools to remain vital, the community must be both involved in and served by the institution. "The focus of change must be on all agencies and their interrelationships, but education has a special obligation to help lead the way in partnership with others" (Fullan, 1993, p. 6).

The following two chapters specifically describe programs that provide avenues for community involvement in the schools and, in turn, provide the schools with opportunities in the community.

# The Community's
# New Role in K-12
# Education

In fulfilling the special obligation that Fullan (1993) notes that schools have to lead the way in partnership with others, a variety of programmatic structures currently exist. All the programs that are discussed in this chapter are examples of school-community partnerships. All involve the school and the community working together on various aspects of education and community improvement. These programs are curriculum driven, initiated by the schools for the purpose of improving and augmenting traditional school offerings. The focus of these initiatives is enhanced learning for K-12 students, including enhanced academic achievement. The uniqueness of the communities in which partnerships have developed has resulted in a wide array of partnerships that differ from community to community. In spite of their differences, however, these partnerships are not necessarily wholly discrete programs; rather, they frequently have some elements of overlap, depending upon points of origin, program definitions, and the community's responsiveness to the initiative.

## Volunteers

Schools, like other service providers in the community, find themselves facing increasing demands with declining resources. Compounding this situation is the depersonalization of services that occurs when there are not sufficient human resources to address client needs. The effective use of volunteers is one strategy for personalizing and expanding services of the schools in a way that is meaningful to both the client and the service provider.

School volunteers are individuals who contribute their time and talents to further the goals of the educational system. The level of contribution depends upon the volunteers' interests, skills, and availability. Winecoff and Powell (1976) categorize school volunteer assistance on the basis of time and location of service. One-time volunteers are those who provide 1 day or less of service, such as a guest speaker for a class. Short-term volunteers provide 1 day or more of service over a limited period of time (less than one semester); an example would be an instructor for a minicourse in photography. Long-term volunteers provide service on a regular basis over an extended period of time; an example would be a media center volunteer. Although these are examples of on-site volunteers, there can also be off-campus volunteers who work at home on school-related projects, such as someone who helps develop instructional materials for the teaching staff.

Asche (1989), in materials prepared for the National Association of Partners in Education, notes that volunteers can serve education in a variety of ways. Specific roles for volunteers include the following:

- General assistance—generic assistance through help with regular school activities
- Intergenerational programs—general assistance provided by older citizens
- Tutoring programs—academic assistance provided to students both during, and before and after, the regular school day
- Resource banks—specialized assistance through topical presentations for the classroom

- School-community partnerships—formalized support for school programs by community agencies or businesses
- Corporate released-time programs—general assistance from local company employees provided at corporate expense
- Career exploration/employability skills/shadowing programs—short-term, off-campus, specialized assistance to students in occupational areas of interest
- Mentor programs—long-term, off-campus, specialized assistance to students in occupational areas of interest
- Special programs—formalized supplementary programs integrated into the school curriculum
- After-school student contact—nonacademic support services following the regular school program
- School staff recognition—organization of recognition events for teachers, principals, and other members of the school staff
- Advisory/decision-making groups—service on various school-based input committees (pp. 50-51)

Everyone involved in volunteer settings benefits from the interaction. Students gain in a variety of ways, including one-on-one support from interested adults as well as exposure to new curricular content. The school gains through having assistance in the delivery of its program and through having a broader base of support from community members who have firsthand knowledge of the school and its program. The individual volunteers have an opportunity for rewards and personal satisfaction that come from work with children and the school staff. In addition, because they represent various segments of the community, volunteers are in a unique position to connect the school and the community through meaningful two-way communication.

The components of a successful volunteer program begin with the planning and development of its overall design, including goals, objectives, and specific activities, under the leadership of a program coordinator. Clear policies regarding appropriate use of volunteers, expected levels of commitment, roles, and responsibilities are put into place. A formal assessment of staff needs and volunteer interests and skills is conducted, followed by the pairing of these needs with identified interests and skills.

Throughout this process the need for good communication is apparent. Feedback provides the opportunity to measure accomplishments against program objectives. Planning, supervision, and evaluation of the volunteer program, as well as of the performance of individual volunteers, are critical to the success of the program. Ongoing recognition of volunteer efforts and of the contributions made is necessary to keep motivation levels high.

Another major component of a successful volunteer program is teacher input and training. A good place to begin is with the awareness of how to use volunteers in a productive way. Teachers and other school staff address issues of confidentiality, commitment, and time expectations that are involved with using volunteers. Building on this needs assessment and increased awareness, the teacher training phase also requires commitment of time to get to know the volunteer and his or her skills. Specific strategies for using the volunteer's talents in the school setting are outlined. Appropriate resources and support for the volunteer's service are necessary and may require leadership involvement. Regular acknowledgment of the volunteer's role in school-student success provides an ongoing incentive for volunteer efforts.

Orientation of the volunteer to school and classroom policies and procedures is the first step in volunteer training, the third component of a successful volunteer program. Clear delineation of the roles and responsibilities of the volunteer, as well as those of the professional (paid) staff, is essential. Specific training for identified volunteer roles may be necessary and may require additional support. The most important area for assessment and training for all volunteers is that of human relations skills. Some of the most fundamental of these skills are oral communication, demonstrating respect and understanding, and listening skills.

Support for the volunteer can come from various community groups as well as from the school district. In situations where there are formalized relationships, sponsoring agencies provide human and financial resources. In informal relationships, support is possible from grants, in-kind contributions, and auxiliary school-based groups such as the parent-teacher association and booster groups. Once the leadership is in place and general procedures are developed, volunteer programs require minimal financial support.

Two exemplary programs using volunteers are in Boise, Idaho, and in the Carman-Ainsworth School District (Flint, Michigan). These volunteer programs are administered by the community education programs in both districts. The program in Boise began in 1970 and uses volunteers in all facets of academic programs for adults, and enrichment and recreation programs for both adults and youth. Volunteers, many of whom have been working in the Boise program since its inception, serve as instructors for various programs as well as staff for program support.

Highlights of the volunteer program in the Carman-Ainsworth district include a strong emphasis of service in the K-12 program at all levels, from Head Start aides and classroom tutors to armchair historians and storytellers. Currently, there are 1,500-plus volunteers contributing more than 34,000 hours of service per year in this suburban-urban district.

Use of volunteers in the school is a broad vehicle for promoting the concept of community involvement in schools. More specific models of community volunteerism are described in the other sections of this chapter. School-community partnerships, community service learning, school-to-work initiatives, and full-service schools are the formalized programs outlined.

## School-Community Partnerships

The 1980s and 1990s have seen the rise of a large number of formal relationships with external entities, both corporate and public-sector agencies. These partnerships have included a variety of models and various degrees of involvement. In the case of the private sector, these partnerships have evolved from ones that were developed to support reform, both conceptually and financially, to the current model wherein the private sector expects the schools to respond as if they were "suppliers" for the corporation's final products. In the case of the public-sector partnerships, there has also been an ongoing emphasis on support for reform, but that support has been somewhat more conceptual and collaborative in nature, especially with respect to the delivery of services. Recent years have seen this commitment deepen and broaden across many facets of these organizations.

Earlier discussion concerned the broad range of community involvement activity with schools, whereas the current focus is on partnerships with formalized structures. "Partnerships are formal, voluntary relationships between the schools and their communities for the purpose of educational improvement. Partners match available resources with identified needs to meet mutually agreed upon goals and objectives. All partners benefit" (Partnerships for Education Task Force, 1989). The benefits for schools are

- Improved community support—personal, financial, and legislative—for education
- Additional instructional resources—materials, equipment, and personnel
- A more relevant curriculum—experiential learning, expanded content, and real-world exposure
- Greater student motivation to stay in school and graduate
- Better career information for students—greater awareness of and access to job opportunities and placement
- Increased opportunities for school staff development
- Growth in mutual understanding of challenges confronting all partner organizations
- Expanded use of school facilities and resources to include the entire community. (Oakes & Thomas, 1991; Partnerships for Education Task Force, 1989)

The benefits for community partners are

- Improved community relations inside and outside the organization
- More efficient use of tax monies and other community resources, including school facilities and equipment
- Growth in mutual understanding of challenges confronting all partner organizations
- Greater stability in neighborhoods where collaborative resources serve the community
- Better informed consumers, voters, and community members

- Employee satisfaction from working more closely with community needs
- Increased assistance with staff development and customized training programs
- Better prepared workforce, resulting in greater productivity
- Better understanding by young people of how community structures work together for common goals. (Oakes & Thomas, 1991; Partnerships for Education Task Force, 1989)

The scope of school-community partnerships varies, depending on the level of the organization at which the commitment is made; the resources available to the partners, the level of need in the community, the degree of personal and organizational commitment, and the demographic makeup and political milieu of the community. Thus partnerships take many different forms.

An exhaustive list of all possible school-community partnerships is impossible. Suffice it to say that these partnerships can be relatively limited or very broad. Classroom tutoring, summer jobs, guest speakers, and incentive programs are examples of limited collaborative agreements worked out between schools and community groups. More comprehensive opportunities for collaboration are found in long-range planning groups, shared staff development training, site-based management committees, and internship placements. These latter examples require complex and interrelated collaborative arrangements, as opposed to the simple and limited ones described in the first listing.

Certain factors are critical in developing effective school-community partnerships. The following is a chronological listing of these elements:

- Willingness to investigate nontraditional delivery systems and create flexible structures for involvement
- Clarity and agreement on the purpose and scope of the partnership
- Congruence with organizational missions
- Organizational commitment supported by appropriate personnel and financial resources from all partners
- Representative governing board and appropriate advisory groups with regularly scheduled meetings and necessary group process training

- Development of trust relationships among partners
- Assessment of community needs and resources
- Development of mutual goals and objectives, roles, and responsibilities
- Assigned leadership from all partners
- Establishment of needed programs
- Evaluative processes for measuring success and providing publicity and recognition

Support for school-community partnerships begins with the personal investment of time and energy on the part of committed leadership. Following initial discussions, when ideas become reality, adequate financial resources are required. Besides the obvious sources of the partners themselves, other sources of support include various governmental agencies, private foundations, and fund-raising within the community. Some communities have developed community foundations and endowments that provide permanent funding for collaborative programs and activities.

The San Antonio, Texas School District has many different types of partnerships that are exemplary because of their comprehensiveness and their broad base of support. Some of the many partners that collaborate with the San Antonio Schools include the Jewish Community Center, which houses daytime programs and offers free child care for participants in the English as a Second Language program; the neighboring district of Alamo Heights Independent School District, where enrichment classes are offered in local neighborhood schools; and the Central Park Mall, which provides space for an adult learning center.

Exemplary programming is available for the Birmingham, Alabama community as a result of extensive school-community partnerships. Especially noteworthy are partnerships with community service agencies and business and industry that have resulted in the National Issues Forum, which brings community residents together to discuss significant current issues; Camp Birmingham, which is a summer academic and enrichment experience provided for city youth to gain experience in hands-on education and workplace skills; and on-site programs for employees, including English as a Second Language, Adult Basic Education, and GED preparation.

In summary, Oakes and Thomas (1991) state that "a successful partnership should enhance a student's knowledge and outlook and should also serve the . . . partner's needs" (p. 12). Through such collaborative programs, schools are able to provide more comprehensive and relevant programming, and partners have an avenue for effective involvement in school reform, while being able to address their own organizational needs.

## Community Service Learning

Although learning through community service has long been a part of public schools' informal curriculum, only recently has community service learning been formally recognized as an important element in student development. This formal recognition came about primarily because of recent federal legislation. In the process, schools have acknowledged that community service is, as Gill (1992, quoting Rolzinski) notes, in the "best tradition of our democracy—dynamic, diverse and decentralized" (p. 2).

Community service learning "constructs real, experiential links between school subject matter and the real world, and in ways that change young people" (Kinsley, 1994, p. 42). It has two aspects: It is formally related to the academic program, and it results in positive benefits for individual students and the community (Kinsley, 1994). Specifically, community service learning

- Enhances academic performance
- Builds critical-thinking skills
- Promotes a caring school climate
- Improves self-esteem and self-concept
- Teaches leadership skills
- Develops a service ethic
- Provides career exploration (Michigan Department of Education, 1992, p. 7)

In brief, community service learning provides real-life experiences and opportunities for students to apply academic learning in a way that makes a difference to the student and to the community.

Community service learning takes many different forms, depending upon its duration, location, scope, type of contact, relationship to the curriculum, and point of origin (Toole & Toole, 1994). The academic needs of the students and the needs of the community come together to shape the individual forms of community service appropriate at any given time in any given community. Thus, for example, several students may be working as a group with a recreation program for handicapped children at a nonschool site. This project provides opportunities to use skills taught in physical education classes, over an extended period of time, in cooperation with a program started by the parks and recreation department.

Effective community service learning begins with institutional commitments on the part of the school and on the part of the community. Policy boards need to clearly state their organizations' support for the program and processes needed. When they do, closer relationships between participating organizations and the schools are nurtured and enhanced. The role of the administrator is to encourage staff in their outreach to the community, provide information on potential opportunities, and facilitate program activities.

Teachers and other adults involved in direct program delivery require training and the necessary financial support to implement their commitment to community service learning. Time is provided for program leaders to reflect on, and grow in, their skills of working together and providing feedback to students and colleagues. Students are encouraged to be reflective learners, to understand the people with whom they are working and what has contributed to program successes, as well as challenges ahead.

Students involved in community service learning are motivated by a belief in the value of their service and in the expectation that it is making a difference in the community. Decisions about participation are made by students within the guidelines provided for the program. Many times these decisions are based on personal interests, social groupings, and perceived incentives such as academic credit.

The best community service learning projects are those that have discernible outcomes, such as reading improvement as a result of tutoring in the after-school program, or a usable playground because of a community cleanup project (Harrington & Schine, 1989). Less tangible, but nonetheless valuable, results stem from the "helping" relationships that develop among and between the students and the community participants. Annual community-wide recognition events typically held at the end of the academic year provide an opportunity to acknowledge the contributions resulting from student participation.

Community service learning projects often require additional financial resources. When seeking this support, Follman, Watkins, and Wilkes (1994) suggest, start close to home by thoroughly using resources within the school and local area; get others involved, especially local service groups; be creative in the use of available resources through in-kind contributions; seek external funding from local, regional, and national sources; and be persistent in the search. The ultimate goal in seeking long-term support for community service learning is to make it a part of the K-12 curriculum and the general school fund.

Examples of model projects in community service learning are found throughout the country. Additional information about specific programs and about the initiation and organization of community service learning is available from the National Service-Learning Cooperative. This is a clearinghouse set up to provide leadership, knowledge, and technical assistance to support and sustain community service learning programs. It can be reached through its toll-free number: (800) 808-7378.

Community service learning is strongly emphasized in the schools in Minnesota. Especially noteworthy is the program in the St. Louis Park secondary schools that is integrating community service learning across the curriculum, interweaving core courses with multidisciplinary service requirements in community agencies, such as nursing homes. Conflict management training for adolescents is also facilitated through partnership with adult leaders in the community in a service learning format.

The state of South Carolina recently awarded funding to the community of Charleston to implement community service learning programs. The result is Learn & Serve Charleston, administered by the nonprofit organization, Youth Service Charleston, and the Charleston County School District. The project promotes service as a learning activity and integrates service into the academic curriculum. Students select the curricular focus, and a team of teachers and trained consultants assists in identifying appropriate community service learning experiences to meet learning objectives. Summing up all the benefits of community service learning, Kinsley (1994) asks and answers the following key question:

"Why should we involve our children in doing things like this? Two quick reasons: One is that they get a better education—they learn better, more broadly, and more deeply than in the classroom alone; the other is, it changes them as human beings." (p. 41)

Community service learning is one of the most effective strategies for community involvement and gaining support for schools. It is a powerful experience in what can happen when we address mutual benefits.

## School-to-Work Initiatives

School-related programs that address school-to-work transition are included in the term "school-to-work initiatives." Stern, Finkelstein, Stone, Latting, and Dornsife (1995) equate "school-to-work with school *for* work—that is, education and training programs in which preparation for work is explicitly a major purpose" (p. 9).

Schools have a long history of delivering programs focused on preparing students for a world of work. Beginning with the Smith-Hughes Act of 1917, and further developed by the Carl D. Perkins Vocational Education Acts of 1984 and 1990, the federal government's role has been to actively promote a variety of school-work initiatives through the schools. Programs resulting from these initiatives include cooperative education, apprenticeship programs, vocational and technical education, and various industrial training programs. Each of these programs begins with schools attempting to provide career options for the non-college-bound student by seeking the cooperation of business and industrial partners.

The School to Work Opportunities Act of 1994 marks a major change in federal vocational legislation because of the new systemic nature of the relationship between schools and the workplace that is fundamental to the legislation. Business partners are required to be formal, active role players even in initiating the collaborative activities funded by this act, thus changing the nature of the collaboration. Further, although many of the earlier education reform efforts focused on academic programs, this legislation represents the educational reform effort as focused on what were traditionally non-college-bound youth.

Three core elements included in the current School to Work Opportunities system are

1. School-based learning—includes career awareness and career exploration and counseling, challenging academic standards and skill standards, coherent multiyear sequence of instruction, and regularly scheduled evaluations of progress
2. Work-based learning—a planned program of job training and experiences relevant to the student's career and leading to the award of a skill certificate, paid work experience, workplace mentoring, and instruction in general workplace competencies
3. Connecting activities—to ensure coordination between school-based and work-based learning components (Michigan School-to-Work Partnership, 1994, p. 2)

A combination of these elements results in integrated school- and work-based learning by means of a combined curriculum and a planned link between secondary and postsecondary education.

Students, educators, employers, and government and community groups all benefit from collaborative school-to-work programs. For students there is a greater range of occupational and educational opportunities, career counseling, and enhanced prospects for employment after graduation. Because students have actual work experience integrated with academic support, they grow in self-confidence through success with real-life work experience. Postsecondary opportunities are essential to the goals of the programs, resulting in students' potential for future advancement.

Educators benefit from seeing a reduction in drop-out rates and better student attendance because of the relevance of the curriculum. True integration of academic and vocational elements in the curriculum is achieved, resulting in higher employment rates for graduates and better informed choices about college opportunities. Public confidence in the schools' programs is enhanced by the positive results that come from student successes in the workplace.

An expanded pool of well-trained applicants is a major benefit for employers. Involvement in the development of the schools' academic and vocational curricula enables employers to shape the training of potential employees to meet workplace demands. Observation of students in internship and mentoring situations allows for on-site assessment of trainees before hiring decisions are made.

The community at large benefits primarily through stimulation of economic growth, a more highly skilled workforce, and enhanced employment levels for the local citizenry. Also, the community perceives that there is higher quality and greater relevance in the schools' programs, a perception that augments community confidence and pride. Thus the quality of life in the community is improved.

School-to-work initiatives are commonly classified into two categories, both of which include linkages between secondary and postsecondary education as a part of the collaborative relationship with business and industry.

- School-*and*-work—students work and attend school at the same time. Examples of this type include cooperative education (paid work for students in their field of study) and apprenticeship programs (experience toward occupational certification).
- School-*for*-work—students have academic preparation for specific work as part of the mission of the school. Examples of this type include vocational education (job-related training), school-based enterprise (student activities resulting in goods or services for sale), tech-prep (4 years of articulated, sequential course work leading to an associate degree), and career academies (combined personal, academic, and vocational training). (Stern et al., 1995)

Development of school-to-work initiatives requires specific elements for success. Primary among these is identification of key leadership in all partner organizations. The process of initiating contacts and securing agreements requires a deliberate brokering effort on the part of some individual or organization. This brokering function is one that is often undertaken by the schools.

After initial agreements are implemented, it is important that there be long-term and ongoing commitment by all sectors. "Top-level leaders should understand that there are no 'quick fixes' and must be willing to assign time, money, and human resources to the partnership effort" (Imel, 1992, p. 22). Those involved in the actual delivery of school-to-work programs—teachers, school principals, vocational education personnel—need to be risk-takers, able to experiment with new configurations of instruction and delivery.

Elements of the program include ongoing career information and guidance that foster self-determination for all students, regardless of academic achievement levels. Life skill development is essential for productive work of all kinds. Additionally, the curriculum in school-to-work programs is both school based and work based. Contextual academic learning is integrated with appropriate work site experiences. Also, ensuring that career awareness begins early in the elementary years provides a solid basis for specific school-to-work experiences in the high school, while providing students with a foundation for understanding "career" as a lifetime growth experience.

The New York City Youth Action Program is an outstanding model of a school-to-work initiative. Beginning with a mission to build leadership and empower youth, the project provides learning opportunities through academic and skill-based training with culminating experiences in the community. Rebuilding abandoned sites for the homeless and developing community advocacy for environmental issues are two areas where students have been providing service to the community as a result of their learning.

The Pasadena (California) Graphic Arts Academy provides training in printing and graphic arts using the school-within-a-school model under the sponsorship of the Pasadena Unified School District. Using teams of teachers and students, and supported by mentors from the Printing Industry Association of

Southern California, the program provides unpaid internships and paid work opportunities for students in a 2+2 youth apprenticeship format. In conclusion, as with any new initiative, creative financing becomes paramount to successful implementation. Charner, Fraser, Hubbard, Rogers, and Horne (1995) state that

> Without creative financing strategies, no high-quality school-to-work transition program can survive. The special requirements of putting together a comprehensive system make it necessary to identify and reallocate financial and in-kind resources from diverse federal, state, and local government agencies; school districts; businesses; community-based organizations; and foundations. (p. 59)

The current school-to-work initiatives change the role of the schools from that of initiator and provider to that of collaborator and facilitator. The shift is to true partnership with business and industry in the development of programs that integrate both academic and vocational activities, providing a system for relevant and future-oriented training.

## Full-Service Schools

> It has long been known that the needs and problems jeopardizing vulnerable families are usually multiple, varied, and changing. Yet, it is equally true that most of our services are organized narrowly to respond to categorically defined problems and are isolated from other relevant needs or circumstances. (Center for the Study of Social Policy, 1993, p. 5)

In addressing the needs noted above, public schools have responded to the call to serve as the focal point for the delivery of a variety of health and human services targeted to support children and families. This concept of using the school for delivery of services is popularly referred to as full-service schools. Although the term "full-service schools" is new, the concept and practice of having the schools serve as brokers of such services has been implemented for several decades in a number of communities across the country under the term "community schools."

Although there is no one predominant model of full-service schools, the term "is defined by the particular community and school, with a mix of services that are needed, feasible to provide in school facilities, and acceptable to the school system and community" (Dryfoos, 1994, p. 14). The focus of services is on early intervention in providing assistance to support the whole child as a member of the family unit.

The full-service schools model provides benefits for schools, for children and families, and for the agencies involved. Schools find more success in providing instructional services when children are emotionally and physically ready for learning. Such success builds public confidence in the work of the schools and thus greater financial support. Children and families benefit by having multiple needs addressed at one accessible location in a user-friendly, affordable way. The potential for students' academic success is enhanced as barriers to learning are removed. Community agencies are able to deliver their services in an integrated, supported environment that promotes efficiency and eliminates duplication. This results in better service delivery at the lowest cost to the agency and the client, thus freeing resources to address newly identified needs and services and enhancing the mission of the agency.

Service delivery can be school based, school linked, or community based. School-based services are those services delivered at school sites, whereas school-linked services are those that are part of an overall delivery plan directed by the school but are provided at a location other than the school—usually near the school. Community-based services are those that are administered solely by community agencies but are often referral sites for problems and needs beyond the scope of the school delivery program (Dryfoos, 1994).

As with the other collaborative efforts discussed earlier, there are specific considerations in planning, implementing, and evaluating full-service schools. The key to initiating this type of collaborative effort is with leadership—leadership of the schools and leadership of the community agencies involved. Major questions to be resolved have to do with governance, commitment, liability, and responsibility. Written agreements that clearly define the purpose and scope of the collaborative effort are necessary.

Issues involved in the actual delivery of services include confidentiality, needs assessment, roles, and coordination. The obvious need to protect clients in the delivery of services requires that all participants, from the governing board level to the service provider, be well versed in matters related to confidentiality. A menu of services is developed after an extensive needs assessment conducted collaboratively by all participating agencies. Because most agencies have a history of providing services in a fragmented and isolated environment, it is important to explore thoroughly the issues of role definition and responsibilities. Participating agencies find the most success in these kinds of partnerships when they are flexible and willing to share information and resources. Coordination of time and space involved in delivery of services is the responsibility of the site-based administrator.

Evaluation of full-service schools is an ongoing process that begins with the development of goals and objectives in the planning phase. Measurable criteria are identified as part of the overall plan for the project and are continuously referred to throughout the implementation stage, with adjustments made as needed.

Financial support for full-service schools comes primarily from the school district and participating agencies. Often national, state, and local governmental resources are available to support collaborative services. Other human resources are available through volunteer programs.

The full-service school concept represents a broadened response to the public's belief that schools should serve the emotional and health needs of students, as well as their academic needs. The 1995 Phi Delta Kappa/Gallup Poll of the public's attitudes toward the public schools reported that 91% of those surveyed felt that it is somewhat important or very important for schools to incorporate this role of service as part of the schools' mission (Elam & Rose, 1995, p. 44).

The national reform effort in delivery of social services has targeted Florida as one of the states to implement pilot programs, whereas the state itself has enacted legislation supporting the development of full-service schools, especially as related to student health. The Family Service Center in Gainesville is a school-based program that provides multiple services for families. Seven specific service areas are included in the center: a health clinic; mental health services; early childhood programs; an adult education learning center; Chapter 1 programs; a vocational education lab; and economic services.

Kentucky also has been involved in major education and service delivery reform and is in the forefront of promoting and funding linkages between school and family service initiatives. Each local school district in the state is encouraged to develop family resource centers with services that include full-time child care for preschoolers, after-school child care, parent education programs, and health services. Approximately one half of the school districts in the state have instituted such centers.

Throughout this discussion about the community's new role in education, the focus has been on improving the learning environment for students. However, in order to truly affect the whole child, it is not sufficient only to address programs involving the K-12 day school experience. Of equal or greater importance in student development is the influence of the larger community, including that of parents and others involved in the child's daily life outside of school. Chapter 4 discusses the schools' new role in lifelong learning, particularly supplemental programs for youth and adults.

# The School's New Role
# in Lifelong Learning

An important aspect of the reform movement in education is the development of mission statements for the school district as a whole and for individual school buildings. These mission statements almost always include a commitment to the development of all children to their fullest potential. Lifelong learning is subsequently mentioned as the support mechanism for addressing the needs of the whole child, because the time spent in the traditional school day is so limited. The challenge to educational leaders is to implement the goals embedded in the mission statement. What can schools do to provide lifelong learning opportunities for these children and the families and communities that support them?

## Supplemental Academic, Enrichment, and Recreation Programs for Youth

Early childhood education programs are the foundation of supplemental learning opportunities for children. There is a growing body of research that has documented both the short-term and long-term benefits of early intervention through preschool and enhanced early school support (Barnett & Frede, 1993). Children benefit academically, socially, and emotionally as a result of interaction with professional educators, peers, and family members in the controlled and supportive environment of programs in early childhood education.

Successful strategies in developing such early childhood programs begin with providing leadership and support for all early childhood opportunities in the community. These opportunities include day care programs, government subsidized initiatives for at-risk children, and other preschool arrangements such as cooperative nursery schools and private-sector enterprises. If early childhood education is provided by the public schools themselves, it is often the result of a need for alternative forms of programming for young children. Through attention to coordination and learning-enhanced programming, schools provide the educational focus that emphasizes the development of the child's potential through these programs.

Youth academic, enrichment, and recreation programs supplement the traditional-day school program. Programs are offered before, during, and after the regular school day, on weekends, and during the summer. By supporting and extending the traditional curriculum, these programs add new dimensions to student learning and provide additional opportunities for practice of skills learned. Although the leadership for developing these programs originates at the central office level, the real work of providing guidance and direction for them takes place at the building level. Thus programming varies from building to building, depending upon the needs of the students and community in the local attendance area.

The most common types of youth academic, enrichment, and recreation programs are based on the schools' curriculum and on current interests and trends of young people. Examples of these include homework hotlines, academic tutoring, Super Saturday programs, youth summer day camps, sports camps, and after-school activities of all types. Latchkey programs are also included in offerings of this type. These are held before and after the school day and provide opportunities for unstructured, but monitored, activities for children in support of parental care.

The Orange City School District in Pepper Pike, Ohio, has developed a comprehensive array of academic, enrichment, and recreational programs for youth. These year-round programs include a balance between the arts and other programs specific to the needs of youth. Especially noteworthy are academic programs for youngsters with special needs and the extension of the K-12 curriculum embedded in these activities.

Alternative education programs are a special form of the regular curriculum provided to meet the needs of some middle and high school students in a setting more appropriate for their learning styles. Another variation in setting and format is found in programs for pregnant teens and young mothers and includes support services such as on-site child care. Both alternative education and pregnant-teen programs provide students with the needed support to reach graduation goals and achieve self-direction. Exemplary programs of this type are the Farmington (Michigan) Alternative Academy, part of the Farmington Public Schools, and the Alternative Education Program in the Salem, Oregon School District. This latter program includes a business internship, leadership development opportunities in business and social service settings, and "Night Line" programs that are self-paced evening courses.

## Academic, Enrichment, and Recreation Programs for Adults

Academic programs for adults have enjoyed a long and rich history in the United States, with offerings from basic education through graduate study. Public schools have been proactive in taking the leadership to identify adult learning needs in the community and match them with corresponding educational resources. For some needs, the corresponding resources exist within the schools themselves, whereas for other needs, resources outside of the school are identified. Adult basic education (K-6), high school completion (9-12), and English as a Second Language programs are frequently provided by the school district itself, though there are some delivery models that use other educational institutions, such as the community college.

An example of a service delivery model that includes both the community college and local schools is located in Wyoming. Eastern Wyoming Community College, in collaboration with local schools in six counties, provides outreach programming in the areas of adult basic education, GED preparation, vocational and recreational classes, and college extension courses. School facilities are used for both enrichment and postsecondary education programs.

The basis for decision making regarding delivery of programs for adults is in the collaborative process that begins with informed and involved leadership. Leadership's role is to guide the process of identifying the most appropriate service provider and delivery site, based on community needs.

Adult vocational education is another form of adult academic training, designed specifically for technical career development. Because school districts have vocational and technical centers for the training of youth, these centers are logical sites for the delivery of vocational and technical programs for adults. These sites are also appropriate for use by business and industrial companies in the retraining of their employees.

Adult enrichment and recreation programs encompass a broad range of activities serving many different segments of the community. The extent to which the school serves as the delivery agent for these programs depends upon the needs and resources of the community. The role of the schools is to assist in the identification of needs and resources, coordinate the delivery of programs by various providers, and develop and deliver the programs as needed. Examples of enrichment and recreation programs are those related to self-improvement, cultural events, and sports leagues. Of special note are the many senior citizen programs developed collaboratively with other community agencies. Senior travel clubs, nutrition sites, and intergenerational opportunities, such as the Retired Senior Volunteer Program, are several examples of these programs, many of which are delivered in the public schools. An exemplary program for senior citizens reflecting these components is administered by the Bedford Public School District in Temperance, Michigan.

Leadership for lifelong learning is a unique role for the public schools. The nature of the educational mission of the schools, the training of those who hold formal leadership roles in the schools, and the public ownership vested in public education all contribute to this uniqueness. As educators look to renewal and reform, adopting the strategies of collaboration for the school's new role in lifelong learning provides a broadened base of support for the future and a guide for the present that is firmly rooted in a heritage from the past.

# The Future of Community-
# School Relationships

The single most critical factor in fostering change in the organization is effective leadership, the type of leadership that is not afraid to take risks, seek out the involvement of others, and hold high expectations for themselves and others in the process (Myers & Robbins, 1991). The structure for schools that has been outlined in the previous chapters represents a major change in the way schools view themselves, as well as in the way the community views the schools. The leadership for this change is a shared responsibility that affects all members of the school organization.

The driving force for major change of this type is the expectation of major benefits as a result. Primary among these is greater understanding of, confidence in, and financial support for the schools and their programs. The public, as the educational consumer, becomes the satisfied educational customer. Directly related to this is the enhanced public relations benefit resulting from new mechanisms for two-way communication between school and community. Finally, with community input used in curriculum development and delivery, there is greater cohesion between community needs and school programming, and hence greater relevance in the resulting school programming.

## Leadership for Change

### Policy Boards

The role of policy boards is to create the new vision and develop the policies that make it a reality. This vision positions the school as a provider of service to the community, grounded in the commitment to lifelong learning and collaboration. The board specifies this new vision in setting job expectations for school employees, building budgets and funding priorities, and designing evaluation systems that recognize programs and processes that foster community involvement.

The scope of the changes embodied in the new vision requires a commitment from everyone in the organization, but the "care and feeding" of the programs and services that result require the creation of a cabinet-level position specifically for this purpose. The budget for this administrative position and its accompanying department is a general fund commitment, demonstrating the central role that community involvement occupies in the new structure.

Another role of the board is to seek active involvement with other service-providing agencies and develop collaborative relationships within the larger community. Such activities promote mutual gains on the part of both the school board and the various cooperating community organizations, as each develops trust for and support from one another.

### Superintendent and Central Office Personnel

The major function of the superintendent and central office personnel is to work with the policy board on the development of the vision committing the schools to community involvement, and in the creation of the structures that put the vision into action. Shared decision making and systematic processes for seeking community input require administrative coordination and general supervision of the program and processes associated with carrying out the vision.

With the creation of the new administrative position by the policy board, it is the responsibility of the superintendent to recruit and hire the necessary leadership and support staff. The goal is leadership through empowerment, which requires understanding, commitment, and confidence in personnel. Time, tolerance for trial and error, and budget support are required to guide the organization through the change process as staff become comfortable with new roles and responsibilities. It is also necessary to provide staff development and training opportunities so that everyone clearly understands his or her role in the new vision. Finally, people are held accountable for their responsibilities in the new structure, thus implementing the evaluation system designed by the policy board.

The superintendent and central office administrators also need to be personally involved with various community groups. Besides serving as advocates for the schools in the community, school administrators create avenues for increased community input in decision making and governance through this involvement.

### Building Principals

The role of the neighborhood principal in the new vision expands to provide leadership for lifelong learning and community involvement within the school and local area. The principal is knowledgeable about community resources and their potential uses in the school. Because of the accessibility of the local building, it is the site for much of the new programming for all community members, thus requiring greater support on the part of the principal. This is especially apparent in building management, because local building use is now likely to increase significantly.

Principals committed to the new vision cultivate community input in decision making. This goal is achieved through such processes as community councils and by having community representation on various decision-making committees. This level of community interface is important because the local building is where community becomes "real" for the school and the school becomes "real" for the community.

As the supervisor of the teaching staff in the building, the principal has an obligation to encourage and support the role of teachers as collaborators with the community in delivering the K-12 curriculum. This support involves working with teachers to develop a community-enriched curriculum, as well as providing financial means for bringing community resources into the classroom and taking the classroom into the community.

## Teachers

School-age children are first and foremost community members. Their educational needs have to be addressed in the context of the entire community in order for their learning to be meaningful. Therefore, teachers in the new vision are aware of and involved in collaborative efforts with other agencies in the community. The role of the teacher changes from that of an individual instructor to a facilitator of a collaborative teaching and learning process. This process involves the teacher as a community-supported team member in the decision-making processes of the school and in curriculum delivery. The classroom is an extension of the community, and the community is an extension of the classroom.

Teachers assume responsibility for integrating community resources in instruction and for facilitating learning experiences beyond the traditional classroom. The results of such practices are increased student achievement and greater relevance to identified needs.

## A Prototype for Action

The following plan is suggested as a six-step process for implementing the programs and processes described in previous chapters. In using this plan, consider the size and complexity of the community in which it is implemented. The plan assumes that the commitment of the policy board to the new vision for community involvement in schools is in place, as demonstrated by a formal statement of interest and accompanied by appropriate policies and procedures.

### Steering Committee

A steering committee is formed, composed of representatives from the following groups: school district policy board, school administrators, teachers, school support staff, parents, government, community agencies, businesses, churches, and other community leaders. The purpose of this group is to determine the feasibility of adopting the community involvement model for lifelong learning. Among the tasks to be accomplished by the group are determination of the level of interest, degree of commitment, and status of financial support for the concept that exist in the schools and the greater community. If interest, commitment, and support warrant moving ahead, the committee recommends formal adoption to the policy board.

### Employment of Key Leadership

The policy board, with representation from the steering committee, moves to employ an administrator to provide leadership for the newly adopted vision for community involvement. This individual is a trained educator who is knowledgeable about both the school and the community. He or she is firmly rooted in the collaborative leadership model, able to relate well to all constituencies, and capable of bringing the school and community together in pursuit of common goals.

### Development of Advisory Groups

The administrator for community involvement processes and programs establishes a framework for community input using various advisory groups. These represent different constituencies within the school organization, as well as throughout the community. The most comprehensive of these input groups is the communitywide advisory committee, the membership of which is similar to that of the steering committee. Other, more focused involvement comes from specialized input groups, such as a senior citizens' coordinating council, early childhood coalition, interagency collaborative, or K-12 curriculum committee. The purpose of these groups is to assess the needs of, and identify the resources existing in, constituent groups.

### Training and Staff Development

Effective group process requires specific training in understanding the scope and purpose of the program, as well as knowledge of appropriate decision-making skills. The responsibility for doing this training belongs primarily to the overall program administrator. The training can take place concurrently with, or prior to, program development. Indeed, it is an ongoing process that needs constant review as groups grow, mature, and change.

## Program Development

Using information gathered through the needs and resource assessment process, program leadership works with the appropriate advisory group to establish lifelong learning opportunities that address identified needs using available resources. In some cases, it is the school organization itself that provides the needed programming; in others, community agencies are the primary programmers. The goal is to maximize the use of community resources to meet community needs.

## Evaluation

Effective evaluation begins with the very initiation of the process and the development of the criteria by which to measure success. These criteria are clearly defined and agreed upon by those involved in the process. This evaluation is multifaceted and ongoing, and addresses both the program and the personnel associated with the process. Both formal and informal strategies are used to assess performance and the extent to which goals have been accomplished.

## Conclusion

Increasing community support for schools, both conceptually and financially, is best accomplished through a planned, systematic, and integrated process. This process begins with the school district's mission statement, which expresses the commitment to community involvement on the part of both policy boards and district leadership; grows through identification of community needs and resources; and matures in the development of programs and processes to meet these needs. Obvious, tangible benefits result from increased human and financial resources now available to meet the educational needs of everyone in the community.

# Annotated Bibliography and References

## Annotated Bibliography

Berla, N., Garlington, J., & Henderson, A. T. (1993). *Taking stock: The inventory of family, community and school support for student achievement.* Washington, DC: National Committee for Citizens in Education.

*This is a training manual that introduces the components of an effective family-community-school partnership. It is helpful in assessing outreach activities and in developing an action plan for improvement.*

Decker, L. E., & Associates. (1994). *Home-school-community relations.* Charlottesville: University of Virginia, Mid-Atlantic Center for Community Education.

*This trainer's manual and study guide was developed for use in school-community relations and community education. Its primary use is for graduate courses; however, sections of the manual may be used for presentations and workshops in the areas of educational partnerships and parent-community involvement.*

Epstein, J. L., & Connors, L. J. (1994). *School, family, and community partnerships in high schools.* Baltimore: Johns Hopkins University, Center on Families, Communities, Schools and Children's Learning.

*This report is on the High School and Family Partnership Project involving six high schools in Maryland that was initiated to study the theories, frameworks, and practices of parent involvement at the high school level. It addresses how schools develop and implement such practices, and how partnerships affect students, families, schools, and communities involved. It is based on Epstein's Six-Step Typology of Parent/Community Involvement.*

Lewis, A. (1986). *Partnerships connecting school and community.* Arlington, VA: American Association of School Administrators.

*This is a practitioner's handbook for developing successful partnerships between schools and other organizations. It presents local, state, and national perspectives, including guidelines for establishing, nurturing, and evaluating partnership initiatives. Many specific local program descriptions are included.*

Watkins, J., & Wilkes, D. (1993). *Sharing success in the Southeast: Promising services.* Greensboro, NC: SouthEastern Regional Vision for Education (affiliated with the School of Education, University of North Carolina at Greensboro).

*This is one of a series of publications on "sharing successes" from the SouthEastern Regional Vision for Education (SERVE) that recognize exemplary public school efforts and practices in the SERVE region. Thirty effective programs are highlighted, including description, needs addressed by project, student-involvement activity, funding sources, project results, and recommendations for replication or adaptation. Names and information for contacts are given for each project.*

Wayson, W., Achilles, C., Pinnell, G., Lintz, M., Carol, L., Cunningham, L., and the Phi Delta Kappa Educational Commission for Developing Public Confidence in Schools. (1988). *Handbook for developing public confidence in schools.* Bloomington, IN: Phi Delta Kappa Educational Foundation.

*This handbook provides an overview of the issue of developing public confidence in schools. Further, it describes specific factors that influence confidence in schools and characteristics of schools with high public confidence. The checklist for developing public confidence, located at the end of the handbook, is a particularly helpful tool.*

Witmer, J. T., & Anderson, C. S. (1994). *How to establish a high school service learning program.* Alexandria, VA: Association for Supervision and Curriculum Development.

*Witmer and Anderson present a complete guide on organizing, designing, and implementing a high school service program. Each of the steps necessary to institute such a program is outlined and explained, concluding with strategies for handling problems and difficulties.*

Wlodkowski, R. (1985). *Enhancing adult motivation to learn.* San Francisco: Jossey-Bass.

*A guide for motivating the adult learner, this book includes both the concepts and the strategies for designing programs that effectively serve the needs of adults as students. The implementation of each instructional strategy is clearly presented, with many practical examples.*

# References

Asche, J. (1989). *Handbook for principals and teachers: A collaborative approach for the effective involvement of community and business volunteers at the school site.* Alexandria, VA: The National Association of Partners in Education, Inc.

Barnett, S. W. & Frede, E. C. (1993). Early childhood programs in public schools: Insights from a state survey. *Journal of Early Intervention, 17*(4), 396-413.

Bracey, G. (1994). The fourth Bracey report on the condition of public education. *Phi Delta Kappan, 76,* 114-127.

Center for the Study of Social Policy. (1993). *Kids count data book.* Washington, DC: Author.

Cetron, M. (1985). *Schools of the future: How American business and education can cooperate to save our schools.* New York: McGraw-Hill.

Charner, I., Fraser, B. S., Hubbard, S., Rogers, A., & Horne, R. (1995). Reforms of the school-to-work transition: Findings, implications, and challenges. *Phi Delta Kappan, 77,* 40, 58-60.

Decker, L., & Decker, V. (1988). *Home/school/community involvement.* Arlington, VA: American Association of School Administrators.

Dryfoos, J. G. (1994). *Full-service schools: A revolution in health and social services for children, youth, and families.* San Francisco: Jossey-Bass.

Elam, S. M., & Rose, L. C. (1995). The 27th annual Phi Delta Kappa/Gallup poll of the public's attitudes toward the public schools. *Phi Delta Kappan, 77,* 41-56.

Follman, J., Watkins, J., & Wilkes, D. (1994). *Learning by serving: 2,000 ideas for service-learning projects.* Greensboro, NC: SouthEastern Regional Vision for Education.

Fullan, M. (1993). *Change forces: Probing the depths of educational reform.* New York: Falmer.

Gill, J. (1992). Community service: A mandate for middle grades. *Dissemination Services on the Middle Grades, 24*(3), 1-6.

Harrington, D., & Schine, J. (1989). *Connections: Service learning in the middle grades.* New York: University Center of the City University of New York.

Hodgkinson, H. (1992). *A demographic look at tomorrow.* Washington, DC: Institute for Educational Leadership, Center for Demographic Policy.

Imel, S. (1992). School-to-work transition: Its role in achieving universal literacy. *The ERIC Review, 2*(2), 21-23.

Johnson, D. W., & Johnson, F. P. (1994). *Joining together: Group theory and group skills* (5th ed.). Boston: Allyn & Bacon.

Keith, S., & Girling, R. H. (1991). *Education, management, and participation: New directions in educational administration.* Boston: Allyn & Bacon.

Kinsley, C. W. (1994). What is community service learning? Children who can make a life as well as a living. *Vital Speeches of the Day, 61*(2), 40-43.

Kowalski, T. J., & Reitzug, U. C. (1993). *Contemporary school administration: An introduction.* New York: Longman.

Melaville, A. I., Blank, M. J., & Asayesh, G. (1993). *Together we can: A guide for crafting a profamily system of education and human services.* Washington, DC: U.S. Department of Education, Office of Educational Research and Improvement.

Michigan Department of Education. (1992). *SERVE-Michigan: Promoting youth and community service.* Lansing: Author.

Michigan School-to-Work Partnership. (1994). *Implementing a state-wide school-to-work system.* East Lansing: Michigan State University, Center for Career and Technical Education.

Minzey, J. D., & LeTarte, C. E. (1994). *Reforming public schools through community education.* Dubuque, IA: Kendall/Hunt.

Myers, K., & Robbins, H. (1991). Ten rules for change. *Executive Excellence, 8*(5), 9-10.

National Opinion Research Corporation. (1993). *General social survey.* Chicago: University of Chicago.

Oakes, J., & Thomas, D. (1991). A sound investment. *Thrust for Educational Leadership, 20*(5), 12-14.

Padak, N., Peck, J., Borthwick, A., & Shaklee, B. (1993). The development of effective educational partnerships: Perceptions from the community, the schools, and the university. *Community Education Journal, 20*(3), 7-12.

Partnerships for Education Task Force. (1989). *Michigan Partnership for Education.* Lansing: Michigan Department of Education.

Ramey, S., & Ramey, C. (1994). The transition to school: Why the first few years matter for a lifetime. *Phi Delta Kappan, 76,* 194-198.

Sarason, S. (1990). *The predictable failure of educational reform: Can we change course before it's too late?* San Francisco: Jossey-Bass.

Sergiovanni, T. J. (1994). *Building community in schools.* San Francisco: Jossey-Bass.

Stern, D., Finkelstein, N., Stone, J. R., III, Latting, J., & Dornsife, C. (1995). *School to work: Research on programs in the United States.* London: Falmer.

Toole, P., & Toole, J. (1994). *An orientation to service-learning.* Minneapolis, MN: National Youth Leadership Council.

U.S. Department of Education. (1994). *Changing education: Resources for systemic change.* Washington, DC: Author.

Winecoff, L., & Powell, C. (1976). *Organizing a volunteer program.* Midland, MI: Pendall .

CORWIN
PRESS

**The Corwin Press logo**—a raven striding across an open book—represents the happy union of courage and learning. We are a professional-level publisher of books and journals for K–12 educators, and we are committed to creating and providing resources that embody these qualities. Corwin's motto is "Success for All Learners."